© David Lyall 2012
All rights reserved
ISBN 978-1-4716-4780-2

Contents:

Cut and Dried
The Lovers
Hiding the dark
Those who
Framed
The Americans are coming
Photos1
The dog died
The phone
Crows
First day
A daughters keyboard
A million acts of resistance
Photos2
Clock
Always
The cycle seat
The way to work
Rita
Cat
Speak

For my family
for their incredible love
and for providing me with so much material over the years…

Cut and Dried

Years of staring at the backs of heads took its toll
and hairspray began to catch the back of the throat.
Day after day the heads came, the hair fell
over the shoulders onto the floor, and thoughts

of all that dry, dead stuff began to choke.
You dreamt of pillows full of tangled hair
and mattresses and duvets, and when you woke
there were scissors in your bed and shreds of cotton
everywhere.

But the phone kept ringing, filling the book
with pages of perms and blow- dries and trims
and more people with photos who wanted to look
"like them." Daily reflections in the mirror grew dim.

Then what you'd run your hands through betrayed
you like a lover, and that which you'd treated like a slave
rose up in uncontrollable tufts, curls laid
themselves flat, perms failed and finally something gave.

The streets seemed full of jagged split ends,
you felt there was serious cutting to be done,
so you tied up some schoolgirls and shaved their heads,
went home and watched the carpet growing long.

Surrounded by heads when the police came,
in the kitchen - heads of lettuce, cabbage, cauliflower,
their leaves carefully trimmed, tidied up, neat. "A shame
to disturb him," the sergeant said as they led you to the car.

A year on and people don't notice you any more,
you're starting to come to terms with what happened,
when women walk past tossing their heads you look at the floor,
and now the sight of scissors doesn't make you too frightened.

With your hands in your pockets you look the same
as anyone else and no-one could guess you'd gone insane,
but certain things denounce you, like those scars that linger,
- the red indented rings round the thumb and forefinger.

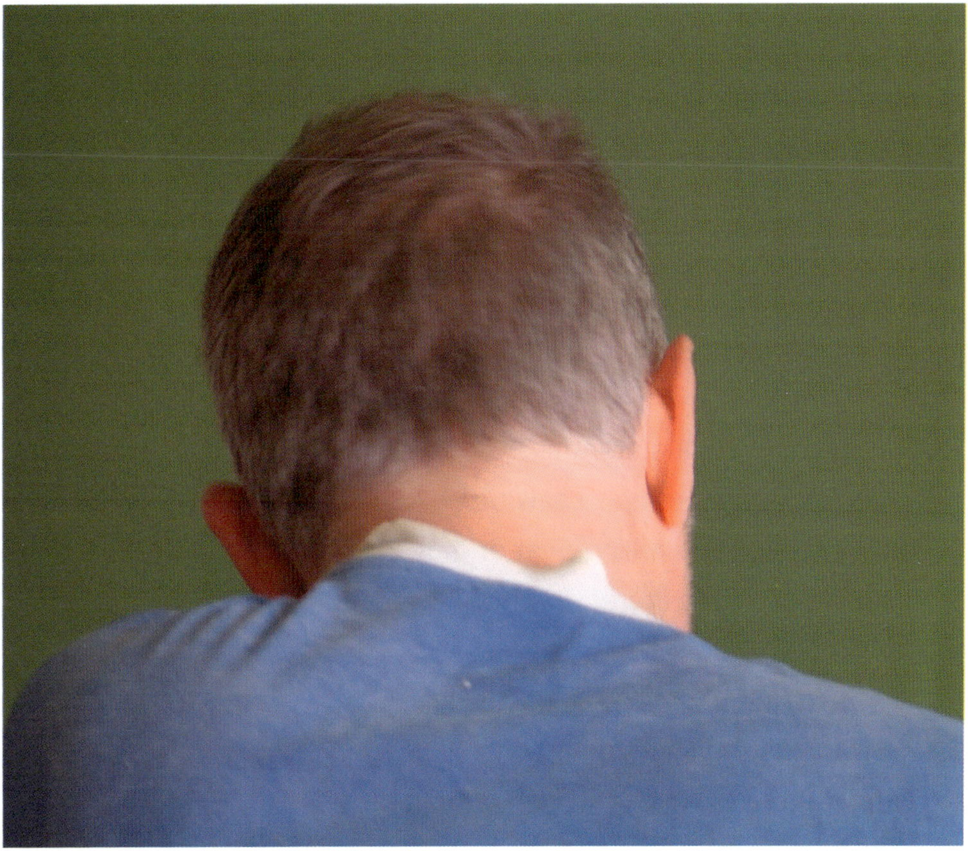

The Lovers

We danced along the front,
we took up the tune of the sea,
tide pushed up beneath the pier,
seaweed hung like drowned men on the beams.

I felt something swell in me.
The moon washed itself in the dark water.

We lay down on the stones
to see the stars but none saw us.
Only the thick sea rolling over and over
watched us move there.

Slowly the night grew cold and cruel,
we watched the lights going out.
Then there was hard water on our faces,
hiding, filling mouths and noses, rushing over.
We held the moons face down in the dark water.

Hiding the Dark

I was hiding the dark inside my head,
others lazy of distraction seemed free.
I was always someone else instead.

Ran my fingers on a name carved in wood:
a sort of love that never happened to me.
I was hiding the dark inside my head.

You heard 'I love you', but what my mouth said
as we lay there together, was lies, each word clearly.
I was always someone else instead.

Wanted my first to be the one I adored,
watched myself fumbling, drunk on the floor,
we were hiding the dark inside our heads.

Meant to avoid the tears, hoped to be true, tried
to be the one who would look after you. But see!
I was always someone else instead.

Felt a hand on my shoulder, a shadow in my tread,
turned my heart round in hope you were looking for me.
I was hiding the dark inside my head:
I was always someone else instead.

Those who

Those who have never grown up
just grow older, forever
teenagers, take washing home to mother.

Stuck in the mind set
of the playground, unchanging, they stay
unchallenged: extended school days.

Housework is the homework
which never gets done, each day
cluttering up like stubs in the ashtray.

Tired out like jokes become
too familiar; have fates
tied down with immovable weights.

Relationships untended,
broken down; how it goes,
feathers to every wind that blows.

Like children, whose
attention strays: would rather laugh
than stare themselves in the face with life.

Like children hate
seriousness, loyalty strains, the friends
who snigger behind their hands.

Framed.

Outstretched, relaxed,
a young woman's hand: neat,
supple, lightly tanned.

Near the open fingers
a blue plastic bottle top, come to rest;
debris: small rocks, powdered brick dust.

The hand unmarked.
But revealed, by the white cotton sleeve,
a seeping stain of blood.

And tight round the wrist
for identification, a black plastic tag
with a number: 10.

The Americans are coming

Smooth out the stars and stripes,
pull them taut at the edges.
Press and fold the tunics
into familiar creases.

Rake over the driveway,
for the uniformed officers come.
Dust down the rosary
one bead at a time.

Amend the constitution
with 'they must pay'
Bury Geneva with a B52.
Stitch up the hoods in Guantanamo Bay.

Close down the market
as if you'll never see food again.
In shock proof boxes pack the museum,
history is being rewritten.

Rouse the hospitals,
empty the old and sick from their beds.
Tell mothers and grandmothers
abandon your knitting.

Push the clouds to one side
with shock and awe.
Let earthquakes tremble
in the face of this terror.

Close the prayer book on a folded page.
Roll up the mat,
take your shoes from the door,
you may never need them any more.
The Americans are coming.

Photos 1

I dreamed my Dad sent me photos
via mobile, from the tops of tall buildings,
the screen lighting up with greenery
and rural peace, where from a church,
a castle, the roof of a school,
narrow roads stretched out between hushed fields.

There was vertigo in them, headiness
where he had leaned out to get the best shot,
over a stone ledge or through an archers slit.
And I imagined him- fit enough to stroll
clear breathed up the battlements-
manipulate the camera with his once numb,
stroke afflicted hands.

But I was too busy to reply.
When I found time there was no record
on my phone of his number -
I could not find Jack Lyall in any memory.

The dog died

The dog died: left you finally alone
after years of children's returning and pets.
The hallway large with quietness- a family home
with bedroom doors now permanently shut.
'That's it for me now, my last one,' I was told,
'too much to invest in such small things.'
Secretly because you felt too old
you were winding down; morbid old age brings
thoughts of the time left, the next room's peace.
Perhaps the figure in your front garden
on the weedy drive by the car un-driven,
might be carrying a scythe, all that must cease.
Pushed behind like the unwanted pet
that secret fear you might not outlive it.

The phone

Those nauseous thoughts kept creeping in
with other people shiny, perfect, whole-
I dreamt my entire front bridge came out
and crumbled when I tried to force it back,
like biscuit, broken in my gaping mouth.
Shapes rose up from a previous life-
death and hurts- unspeakable shadows
looming from depths, darkness accelerating.
Fear seeped in like a weeping stain, like damp,
gripped sudden like cold on a winters night.
The phone bragged chaos in an analogue pulse,
a small vibration in the ear, a fucked up voice
that whispered to my fucked up soul
-though warm love turned my face to the light-
'you'll never keep me out.'

Crows

Cold summer morning, the trees are spattered black
with crow, like something coughed up.
A portent – branches fuss with their heaviness,
so they launch to the houses opposite.

Their world is minute by minute shifting
nearer or further from danger, and flight
is not the graceful soaring of gulls,
but a heaving, black struggle on the wind.

Still they bark out to the spaces,
rasp at the orange fringe of morning,
and clamber over the roofs and chimneys
like soot-blackened gargoyles.

Waking to them, to the scrabbling
of their flight-hobble over the tiles,
and a brief glimpse through the roof light
of heraldic beak or sinister black wing

calls up lives which are short and dazzling.
They have the early daylight mesmerized -
The morning uncovered -a world of death, chaos, evil:
where Birnam Wood never came to the castle.

First day

Tomorrow our son will start school.
He will put his new uniform on:
black trousers, green top.
And he will stand like all kids do,
bolt upright in the living room grinning,
hands by his side, his hair just so:
brown and tufty like a little bear's.

Together we will walk to school,
he will go in and we will return home.
He may not think of us again,
in a day planted among other children,
crayons, pencils, felt tips.
Where words and books and rainbow colours,
and kids rush in a blur, like leaves
blown around the playground.

It will be his day, remembered in scraps later:
green bushes, dark railings, ants on the grey tarmac,
friends' faces, sunshine.
And then it will be gone,
with the other days, piled up behind
like clothes we've grown out of.

A daughter's keyboard

She has small purposeful hands
Which find middle C without fuss,
And set to playing confidently with deliberate touch.
She likes to teach me and note the contrast
Of her quick fingers with mine:
Articulate yet clumsy, forgetful, out of time.
It thrills me she is musical, creative
And I sit in her room listening to her practice.
She plays Scarborough Fair, then lets me try:
Two hands! My wrong notes follow her out into the hall
and drown the mumbling TV downstairs.
Minutes later she returns laughing, exasperated,
The teacher: jabbing down on my hapless fingers:
'Here, here, here!'

A million acts of resistance

Lying on your back gazing at the sky, you feel the short grass
like a thousand fingers on your neck.
It is 1975. The Apollo missions have been and gone.
Space is a hazy dome, cold as the future.
There's a football by your feet, kicked into submission,
- muddy in an honest 70's kind of way.
You seem pinned down like a grid reference.

Home is a million miles away. You might never go back.
Today seems to stretch on beyond its hours.
Tomorrow the sky will unravel, the ball anticipate the kick,
and scudder through the alleyway, echoing
back and forth against the brick.

You do not know how long you have been here,
or how long this may last, only you sense
the sun on your face, your chest rising and falling.
Earlier friends' voices faded over the curve of the world,
huge landscapes of clouds drifted past.

You have become part of the Earth:
a wind tumbles over your darkening shape.
The grass which laid down under you

is returning to life, you feel it move-
a million tiny acts of resistance.
Dampness creeps into the small of your back.

Thinking about this place at night-
alone, under a flat black sky,
silent, reflecting a deserted darkness up-
thrills like electricity. Your legs cramp.
It is excitement, it is fear, strumming
through that pit of your stomach taut as a wire.

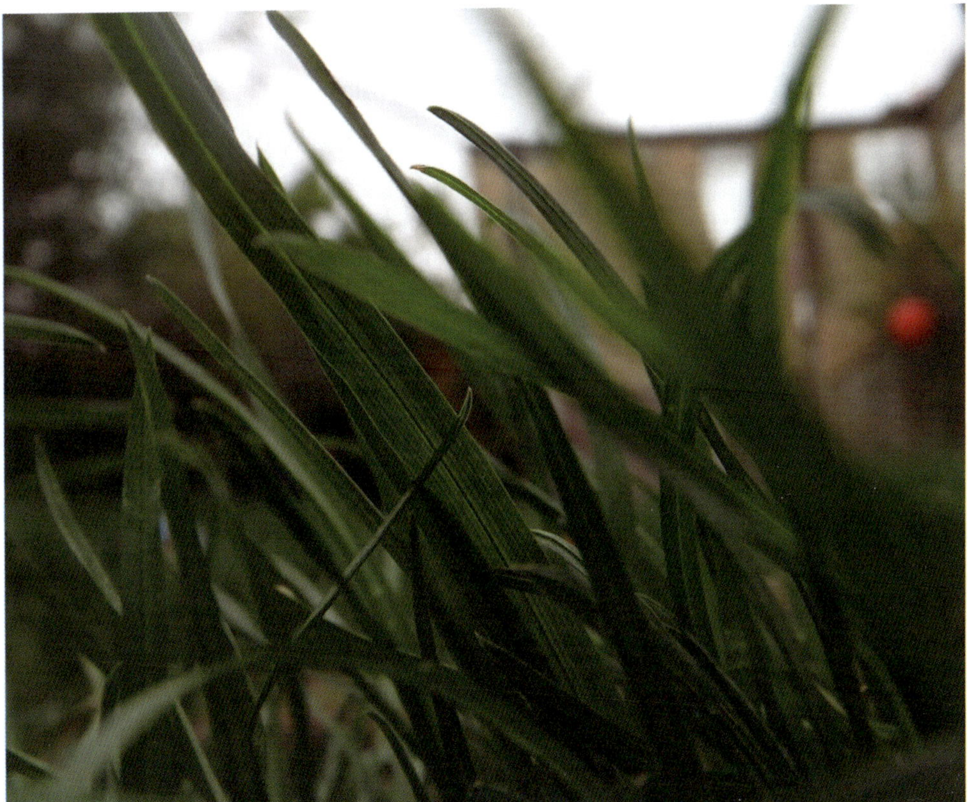

Photos 2

We'd had an empty Sunday,
the kind which settles at the end of summer
like a blanket laid on the bed on cool evenings.
A cloudy Sunday, rain waiting for a signal.
School, which seemed to move away each day of August,
coming back to meet us.

I thought it was a job to keep a kid busy:
sliding old photos into the sleeves of an album
willy nilly- no chronology. But the first pack
spilled open and the frames held us
captive like bright jewels, shining with colours,
smiles, forgotten clothes, old sunshine.

Tumbling out in a glossy waterfall
From the cupboard, bursting from packets,
Each a gentle burning on the retina,
A flashing of synapses, surges in a pulse of memory.
Like minutes on minutes, days on days stockpiled up.
Every street and beach, each bright window, white casement,
lino floor, swept with sunlight.

Sometimes further than memory
Like being presented with new evidence.

Each image an opening of shared secrets.
What your heart had whispered to itself
now said aloud, told, repeated.

Every one a pitch recognized in ourselves,
a perfect echo: how love sounds and replies
until our hearts thrum with gentle resonance.

Like many voices singing.
Like food stored and buried by shared hands in sunshine.
Coming to us on an empty Sunday
To reawaken language in a still mouth.
These things are saved for you.

They will be waiting, to feed an eager hungry heart
In times of hardship, bad weather.

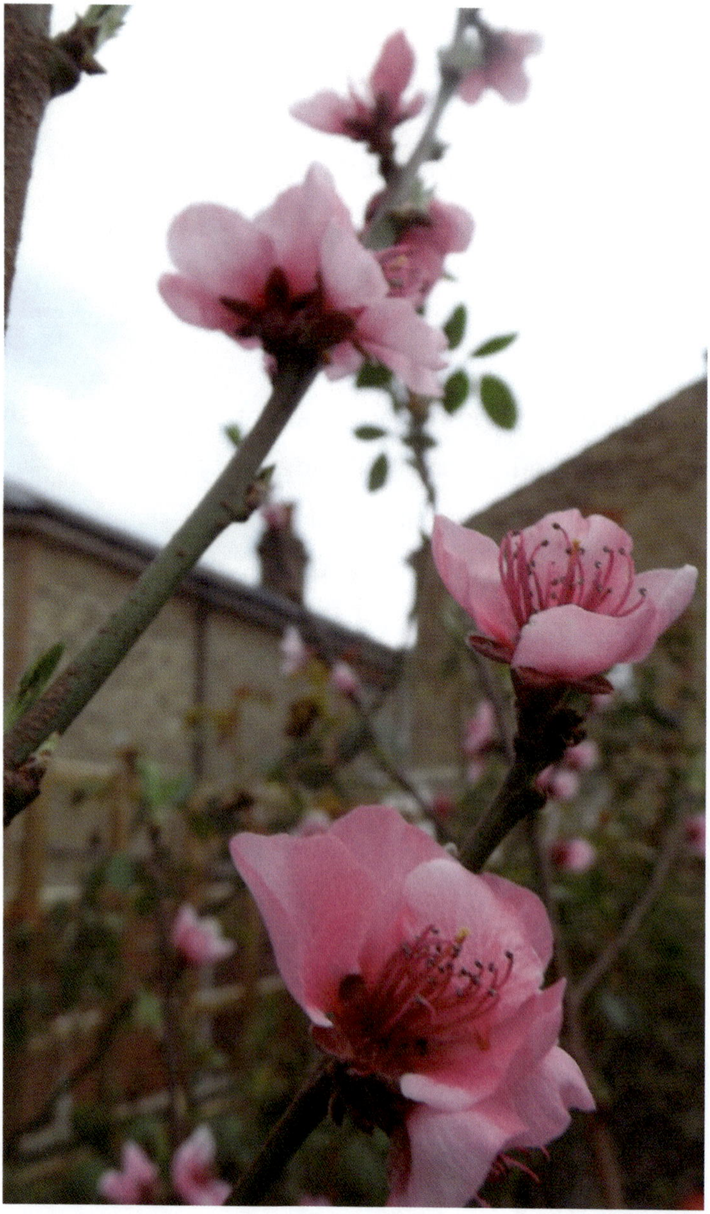

Clock

My dad kept nothing of his parents.

All his childhood was surviving. I mean

living on bare minimum, on what could be scraped together:

Furniture cobbled up from old sets,

mended chairs, cast offs, repairs.

Food had to be eked out, empty stomachs ignored.

They learnt to eat from the fields by season,

to recognize cob nuts, ripened berries,

to not just eat windfall apples but to scoop

handfuls up to ferry home and store.

There never was anything spare

enough to be kept or handed down.

It makes me sad to think of him

doing ordinary childhood things in such slate grey poverty:

pulling on darned socks, washing in cold water,

walking to school with friends in the perishing Welsh winter.

I took his clock, picked up in Fulham in the 1950's, for repair.

Time and a dodgy shelf had seen it finally stopped.

The man in the shop said he'd be inclined
to "throw it in a skip if it were mine."
I explained: it was my dad's clock, I left out
all the stuff about his few treasured possessions,
the poverty and welsh childhood but
he maybe saw it in my pained face.
So he machined it, mended it.

But now the working which kept its mechanism beating
and fluttering like the inside of an egg,
has seized and stopped and will not wind.

My dad wasn't sentimental like I am.
Because his life was welted by abandonment, by grief
and he numbed himself to loss.
I want to hold onto it at all cost.

Because it's one of only a few remaining routes to him,
his memory: that hot, heartbreaking
sense of him at the edge of my mind.
Like his boyhood photo, his stamps,
letters written in his hand
that let me imagine him alive,
nerves and muscles moving,
the hand holding the pen,
holding the key, winding the clock.

His mind playing, his mouth whistling,

his voice saying:

"You want to listen to that bloke in the shop."

Always

Always he put his cup to the left,
hers to the right, and slept on the same side
turned to the centre, his cheek on her neck.
Sometimes he liked to wake early to look at her,
propped up on his elbow, studying the pale colours of her face.

Then fetch tea from the red floored kitchen;
the kettle on the hob, two mugs waiting: his on the left.
And dwell for a moment, listening for sounds of the kids
running up and down stairs, or the TV coming on.

Saturday. Returning to the warm bed made his heart liquid,
like going back to a place without thought,
just sensation, chest rising and falling, a pulse in the throat.

Always he liked it like this:
when love made everything quiet,
when love gave him nothing to say.

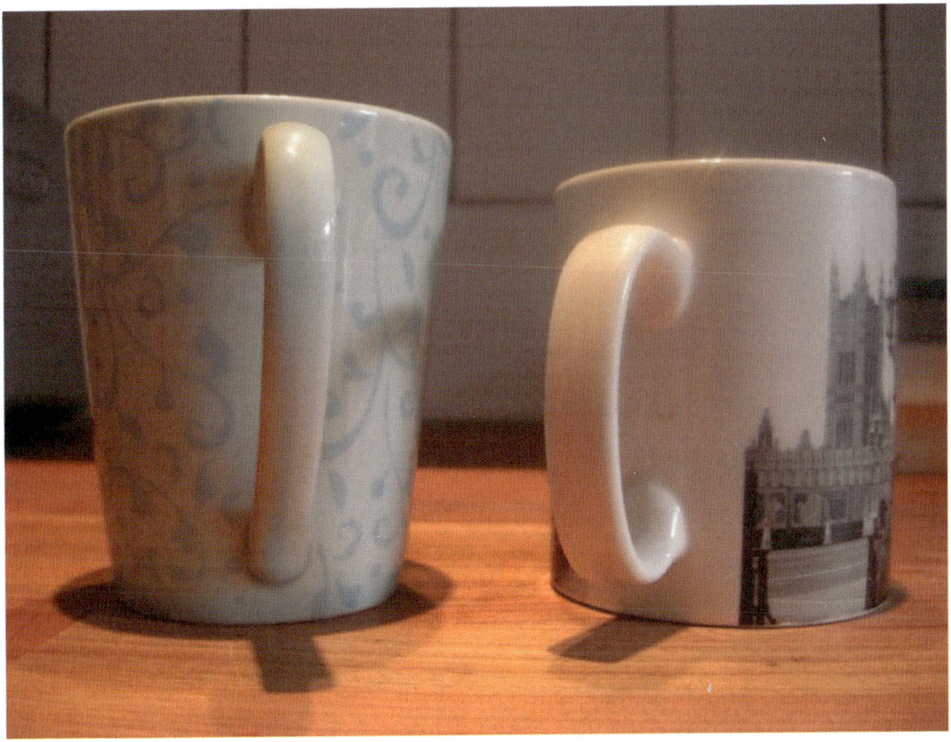

The cycle seat

Cycling up Poppleton Road, the slight incline
to the Tesco bridge, shouldn't feel like hard labour.
But with 20 extra kilos on the crossbar
and hardly able to get my hands on the gears,
I feel my legs burning, a slight shortness to the conversation.
Once over the walkway, it's all downhill- you're done.

One thing you don't see anymore
is people carrying kids on the crossbar.
So we often glide past to odd looks
as if I were dangling my child out of the upstairs window
or leaving them to play in the road.
People smile wryly, nostalgically
like we were pedalling to buy a loaf of Hovis.

It started with nothing at all, bare metal,
but complaints about numb legs
and pins and needles in the feet
meant we needed some cushioning.
So I got an old towel, folded it to a thick rectangle
and fixed it over the crossbar

with a bit of duck tape either end.

(I've seen friends raise their eyebrows
when I say I'm not eccentric.)

My son, clearly impressed, perched comfortably
on the old towel and the duck tape,
whizzing down the back streets past Leytonstone station,
said: "I wonder if the *Dragons Den* would like it?"

Rita

The reservoirs were full today Rita
as I cycled past: two deep blue teardrops
under a huge sky. Mountainous clouds hurried on
and I felt suddenly small and alone.

I looked for you all week, my sister,
as I had once looked for our dad.
And I found the same as then:
a smile, your voice, the reassurance of love,
and the blank hollow of pain.

Against the force of the buffeting wind
for days I had been utterly numb.
Now the sun on my face, the empty sky,
the breath heaving out of my chest,
told me you were gone.

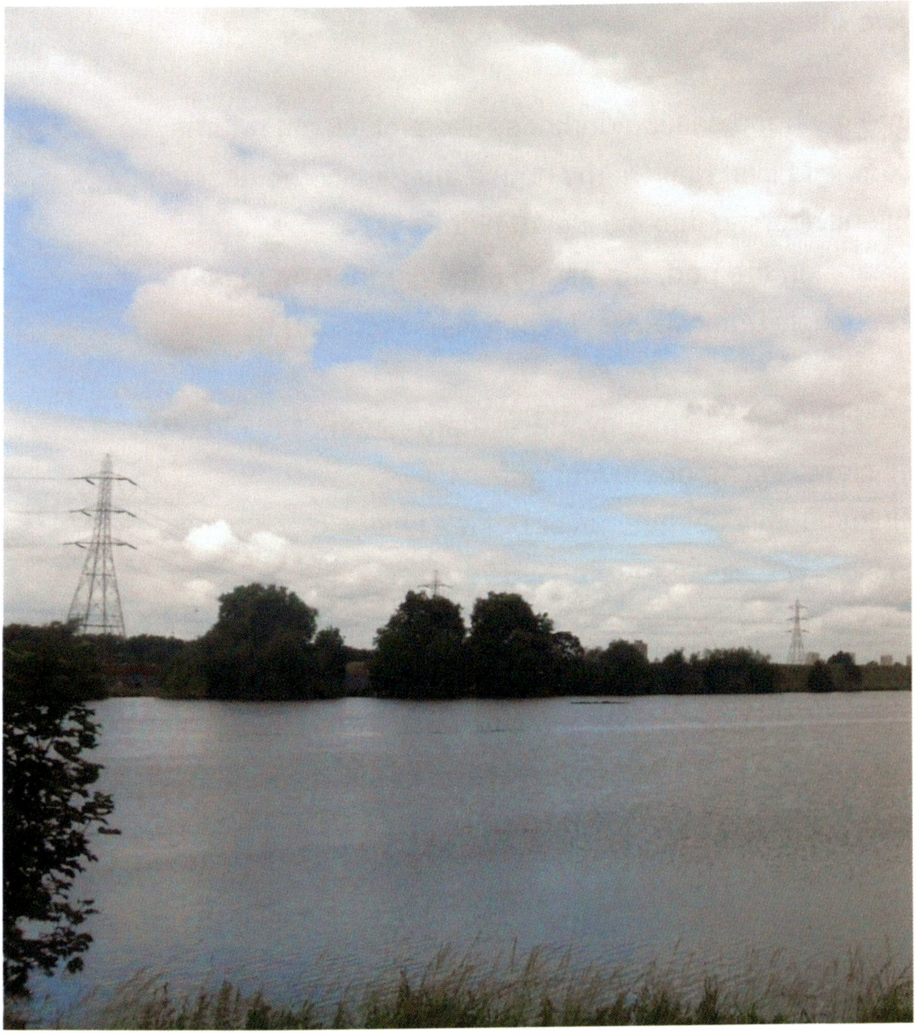

The black cat

Into my head shifting darkness like a black cat returns,
comes to live again in my house after welcome absence.
Silently curling into my life; at night
sleeps on the bed, a presence heavier than its mass,
seemingly unmoveable, its purr a background hum.

This is no gentle moggy. Feral, hard-bitten,
its claws will rip open your guts.
Unloved, this cat has never been a kitten,
this cat will kill your pretty birds.

I've tried to put up fences to keep it out,
yet seen it slide through the smallest crack.
I've learned to recognise the acrid stench of spray
and not let the brain reel and be sick.

It will leave of its own will, any day
I could come down stairs to find it gone.
Meanwhile I have to let it stay,
and somehow sooth the frightened spitting,
feel the claws flex in my lap.

And accept the smoky black slickness of its coming,
and tiptoe through the fragile bones of its killing.

The way to work

Ground rushes under hard rubber tyre,
tread hums, and hums gripping tarmac,
bearings tick to themselves, oiled and free:
a bike following its taut momentum.

Each fissure or divot of expansion or shrinkage,
drain or tree root, rattles through the forks, transmits past pressured air locked in the tubes
up through the spokes and sets a brief ringing in the frame; a creak of sprung saddle,
the leather hard, waxy, not broken in.

This morning bright, crisp as a sheet,
cold but still, good cycling weather.
 A chance to cut through the static air and go at a lick
past the reservoirs on Ferry Lane.
And God you can feel it.
Just the right resistance on pedals,
the gearing good and long, a mild burn warming the legs.
Just the prickling hint of sweat on brow or lip,
some rhythmic song in the head, black road whipping underneath like a spool of film unravelling.

You've done this stretch in rain and sun

against a headwind, with tired legs or tired heart.

And it is a stretch. At Blackhorse Road

the horizon narrows to a point, a triangle laid flat,

industrial buildings on one side, the rail tracks high on the left

the road an undulating typewriter ribbon rolled out.

Lea Navigation meanders under, lapping to the marshes,

Coppermill Lane in the hazy distance.

Today you coast past cars and lorries sat squat,

nose to tail, stuck, but you've been hunched too

over the handlebars on a bad day, like an old man throwing curses to the wind.

Now you're a compass, a gyroscope, your needle driving forward, the world moving under you, around you,

an engineered balance of rubber, metal, bone and flesh.

From a standstill, the resistance bites:

your weight pushing the chain,

your back wheel the little cog,

slowly turning that titanic mass,

the whole globe beneath you.

Speak

Some speak of moving through a spectral landscape,
or the insistence of a black dog come to visit.
Others describe the howling of an arctic winter,
the roaring wind, the shrieking face of anxiety.

For me, after the white out there was dust
like the aftermath of an explosion, that time
before realization: suspended quiet before
the wail of alarms or running of feet.
A dust had come like a charm and settled quietly
over everything.

How that profound dust choked.
Not like the slight honest dirt which rests
almost politely on the edge of a sideboard.
More a heavy persistent smudge,
working into familiar places:
a football game, a workplace, while cycling,
the road itself, the cars and sky all draped
in merciless grey.
A fine silt collected on the faces of children.

At the point of despair, in the numbing
muteness which is mental pain,

we seek to give that thing a name.
We mutter to the silent whiteness, show yourself.
That we might find some tool to begin,
Some language that could whisper in the dark:

"...Here is a lamp, a candle stub.
Here is a stick to beat the dog off.

Here is a tent to keep warm.
Hold on. I will fetch tools, fire, food,
a brush, a broom."

And here I am, in the kitchen, at Christmas 2011.
That's one big cigar, but I think I deserve it.

Printed in Great Britain
by Amazon.co.uk, Ltd.,
Marston Gate.